Start Maths
FIRST STEPS

Counting

Ann Montague-Smith

QED Publishing

First published in the UK in 2004 by
QED Publishing
A Quarto Group Company
226 City Road
London, EC1V 2TT

www.qed-publishing.co.uk

A Catalogue record for this book is available from the British Library.

ISBN 978 1 84835 130 1

Written by Ann Montague-Smith
Designed and edited by The Complete Works
Illustrated by Jenny Tulip
Photography by Steve Lumb and Michael Wicks

Creative Director Louise Morley
Editorial Manager Jean Coppendale

Printed and bound in China

With thanks to:

Contents

Counting 1, 2, 3

Count the sets of pets.

How many dogs have a bone?

Challenge

How many dogs do you think live here?

Counting 1, 2, 3, 4

Count the groups of toys.

Which is your favourite toy here?
How many can you see?

Challenge

Where will the dolls sit?

Counting game

You will each need a counter, and a counter to throw onto the spinner. Throw the counter onto the spinner. Count how many. Move your counter that many along the track.

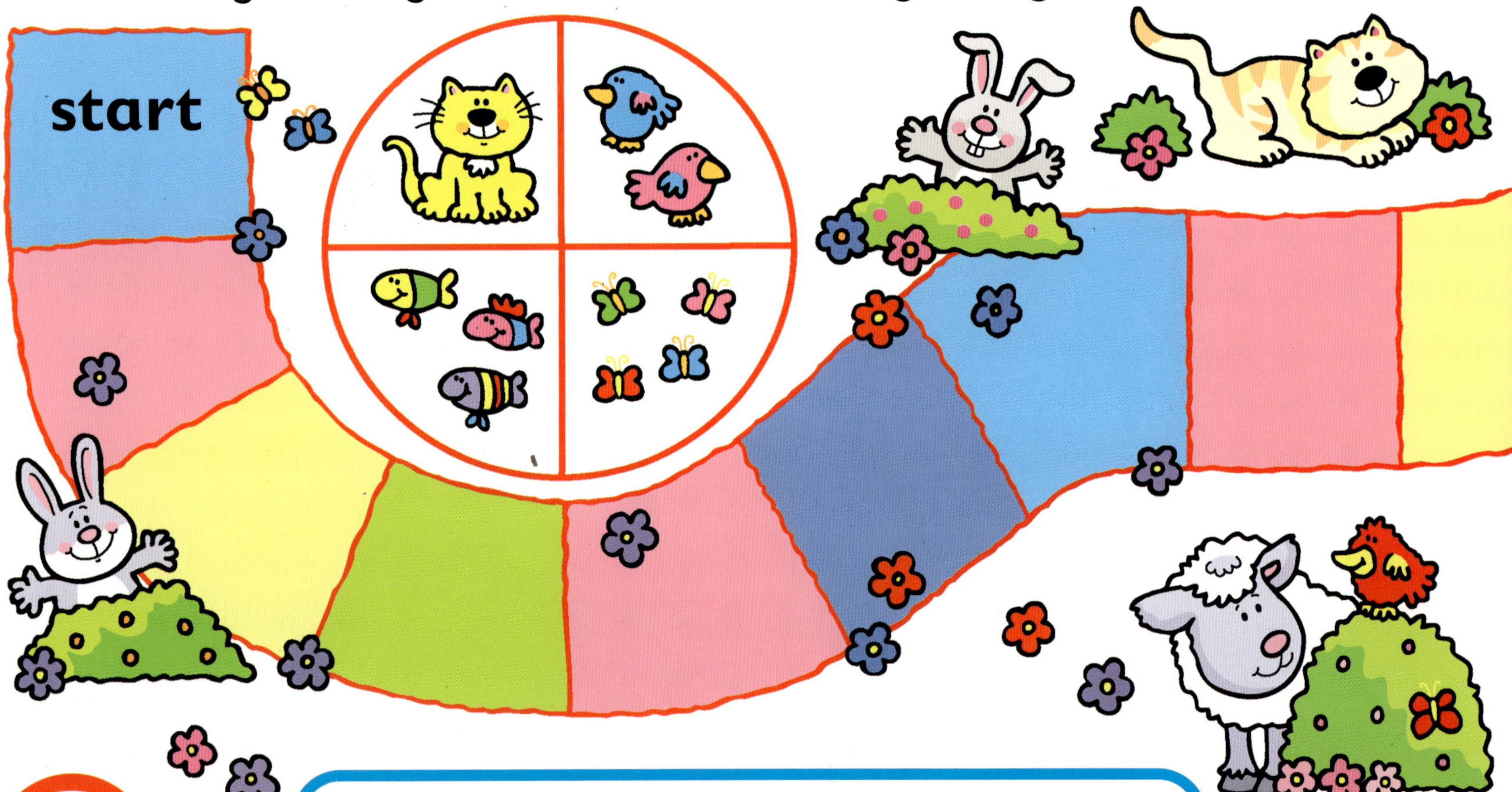

Who will be the first one to the finish?

Challenge

Use a 1 to 6 spot dice.
Play the game again.

Counting 4 and 5

Find all the sets with 4 flowers.

Can you find all the sets with 5 flowers?

Challenge

Draw a garden picture.
Put 4 red flowers in your garden.
Now draw 5 blue flowers.
What else would you like to put in your garden?

Numbers 1, 2, 3, 4, 5

Count the sets of butterflies.

Read the numbers.

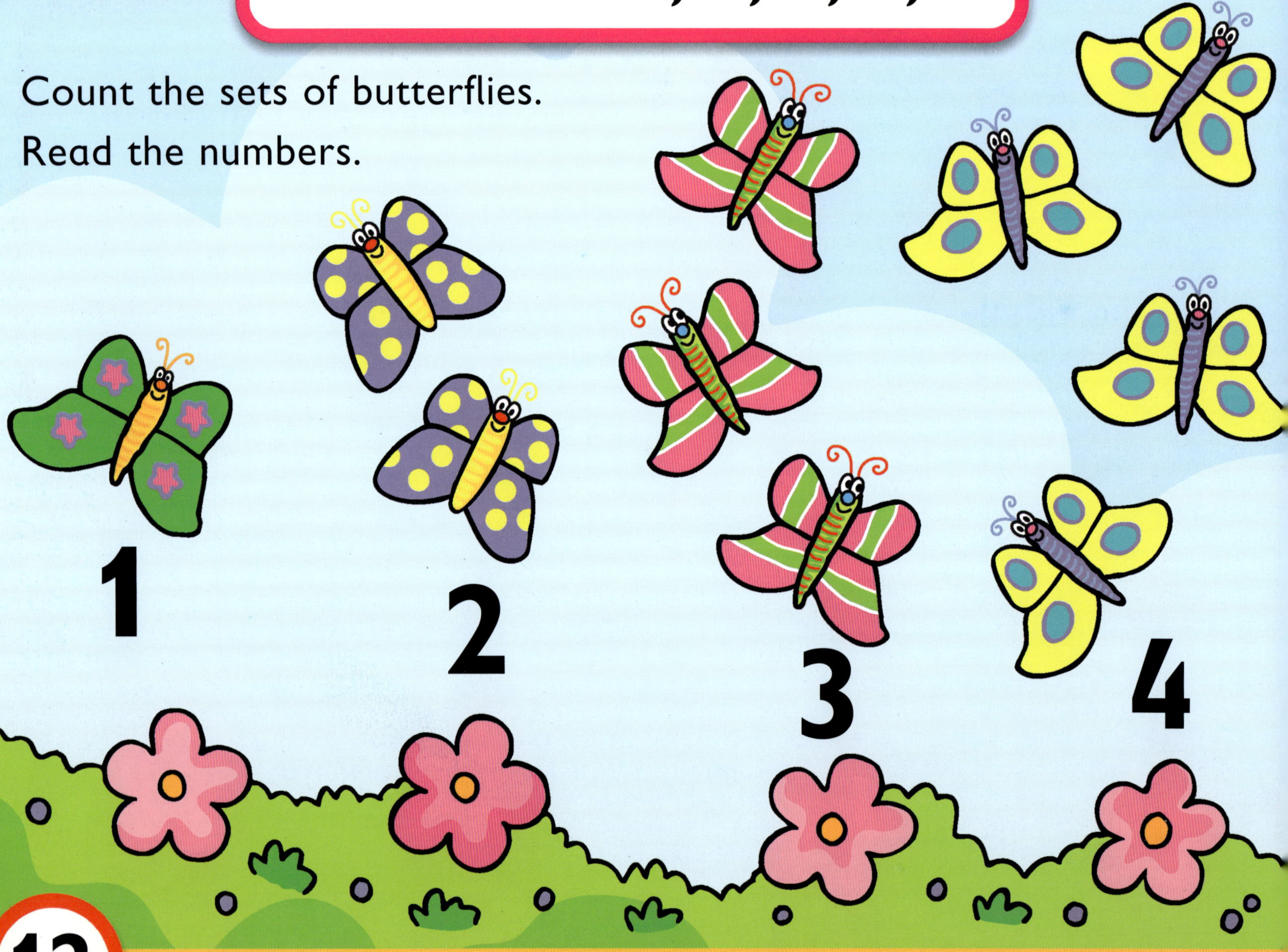

5

Challenge

Can you find page 4 in this book?
Now see if you can find page 5.
What other numbers can you read in this book?

Number matching

Match each set of vehicles to its number.

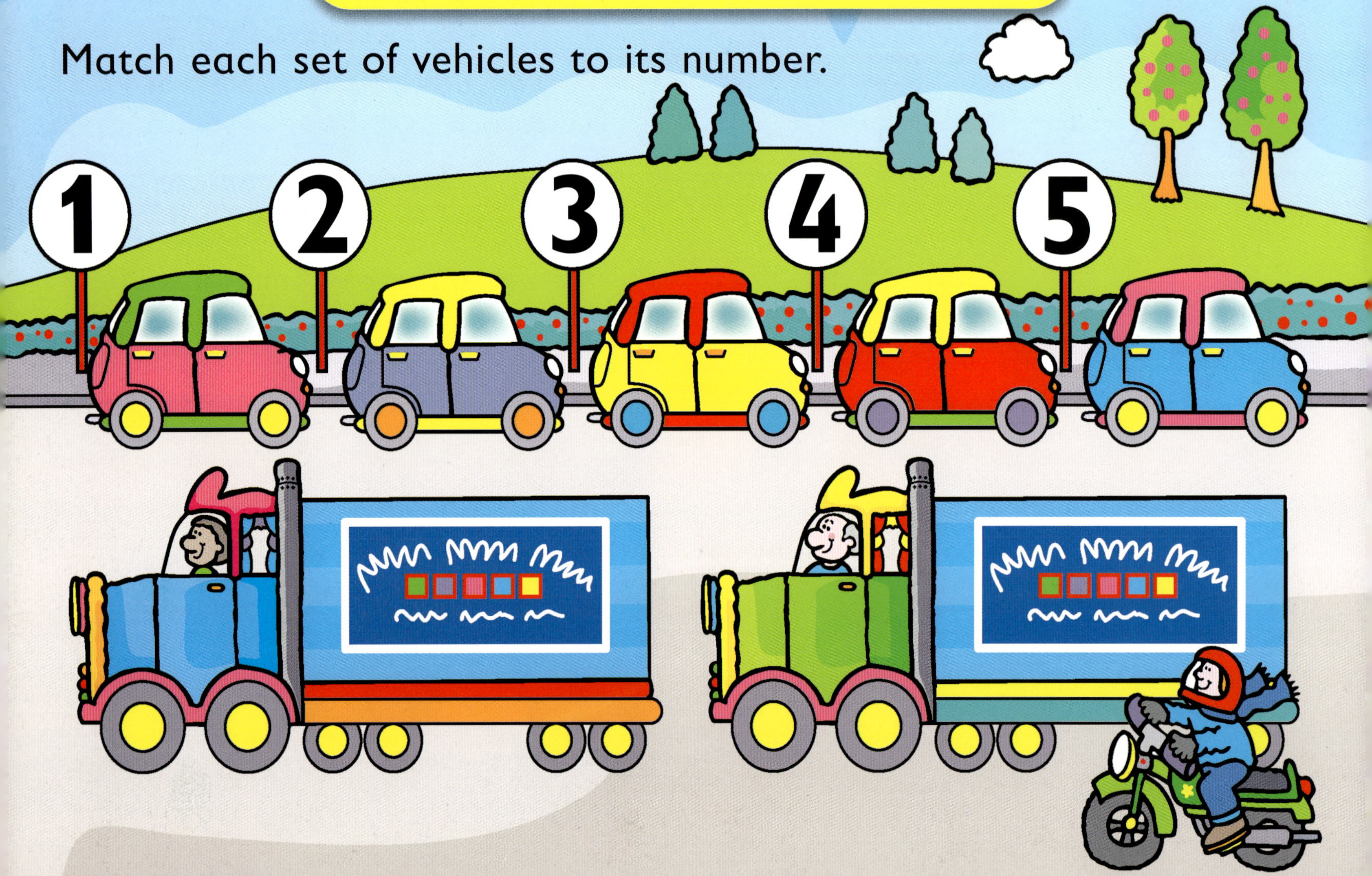

What else can you count in the picture?

Challenge

Look in a picture book.
Can you find 5 different
things in a picture?
See if you can find the
number 5 on a page.

Estimating how many

Don't count yet! Guess how many cups there are.
Now check by counting.

Guess how many plates there are.
Now check by counting.

Challenge

Take a handful of bricks.
How many do you
think you have?
Now you can count
to check.

Estimating game

You will need 5 bricks and some counters to play this game.
Take turns to pick up some bricks. Guess how many you have.
Now count. Put a counter on the number for your bricks.

The winner is the one who covers the most numbers.

Challenge

Take a big handful of bricks. Now count out 1 of the bricks. Count out 2 bricks. Now count out 3, 4 and 5 bricks. Put your piles of bricks in order like this.

I know about 1, 2, 3, 4, 5

Count and say how many.

1 2 3 4 5

Show your fingers like this.

Count and say how many.

Challenge

Find the number 1 in the room.

Now can you find number 2?

See if you can find 3, 4 and 5.

Supporting notes for adults

Counting 1, 2, 3 – pages 4-5

Some children will tell you 'how many' without seeming to count. Praise this achievement. For a child who needs help, offer some counters. The child can put a counter onto each pet, then count the counters, by touching, moving and saying how many.

Counting 1, 2, 3, 4 – pages 6-7

Encourage those who 'know' how many there are without counting. For children who need help, encourage them to touch each toy and count, or use the counter idea for page 4. Ask questions such as, 'Which groups have 2… 3… 4?'

Counting game – pages 8-9

Instead of using the spinner, the children can use a blank dice marked 1, 2, 3, 3, 4, 4. Children who try the Challenge using a conventional 1 to 6 dice will need to recognize numbers to 6.

Counting 4 and 5 – pages 10-11

Encourage the children to count each set. Where children need more help with counting, use the suggestions for pages 4 and 6 above. Ask children who draw a garden how many flowers they will draw, then ask, 'Did you draw … flowers?'

Numbers 1, 2, 3, 4, 5 – pages 12-13

Encourage the children to read the numbers 1 to 5 in the room, on posters, car number plates, etc. They may wish to try to write their own numbers. Do encourage this.

Number matching – pages 14-15

Ask the children to read each of the numerals on the road signs before they match the sets to the correct numbers.

Estimating how many – pages 16-17

Ask the children to guess how many carrots, forks, etc there are, then to check by counting. Use everyday opportunities: ask, 'How many toy cars do you think there are? Let's check by counting.'

Estimating game – pages 18-19

Encourage the children to say how many bricks they think there are, by asking them to look quickly at the bricks and then to look away.

I know about 1, 2, 3, 4, 5 – pages 20-21

Encourage the children to count how many on page 20. For page 21, ask the children to show the same number of fingers as they can see in each picture that you point to.

Suggestions for using this book

Children will enjoy looking through the book and talking about the colourful pictures. Sit somewhere comfortable together. Please read the instructions to the children, then encourage them to take part in the activity and check whether or not they have understood what to do.

Help them to count how many by asking them to touch each picture, then say the number together. Ask questions such as, 'What was the last number you said? So how many … are there?' This will help the children to recognize that counting the last number word aloud will tell them how many there are all together.

When very young children begin to say the numbers, they may not say these in the correct order. Don't despair! With practice, this will be corrected. Saying and singing number rhymes together will help the children to learn the names in the correct order.

As children become more confident with counting, you will probably find that they will look at a group of objects and, without counting them, say correctly how many there are. This is a very important skill that children develop and should be encouraged. Most children can eventually do this for up to 4 or 5 things in any arrangement.

One skill that is begun in this book is that of estimating 'how many'. Encourage the children to have a guess, and remember, no guess is 'wrong'! What we need is for children to become more accurate in their estimates of how many things there are, through practical experience of estimating, then counting to check.